MIND READING

FOR NETWORK MARKETING

HOW TO UNDERSTAND
WHAT OUR PROSPECTS
ARE THINKING

KEITH & TOM "BIG AL" SCHREITER

Mind Reading for Network Marketing: How to Understand What Our Prospects Are Thinking

Published by Fortune Network Publishing
PO Box 890084
Houston, TX 77289 USA
+1 (281) 280-9800
BigAlBooks.com

Print ISBN: 978-1-956171-14-3
Ebook ISBN: 978-1-956171-13-6

CONTENTS

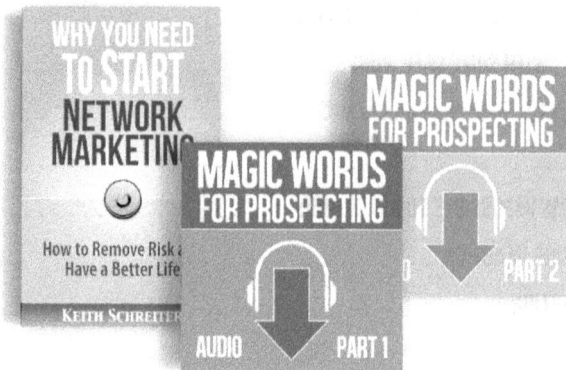

PREFACE

Welcome to the exciting world of mind reading!

As marketers, our job is to understand our prospects' needs and wants. The best way to make sure we serve our prospects is to read their minds. We will have the power of empathy on our side, plus the power of seeing the big picture in our conversations.

Now, we are not magical mind readers (although magical powers would be nice), but we do need to understand what our prospects are thinking and feeling.

When we read our prospects' minds, they connect with us. Now they can hear our message without prejudice. That is all we ask. Why? Because our message is so good that most prospects want what we offer. No pushing, selling, or trickery is needed. They will think, "This is what I want."

Mind reading allows us to customize our message to the conversation prospects have inside of their heads. We know what they want. We know what they are thinking. No guessing. No long time-wasting sales presentations and countless follow-ups. Let's enter their conversation in progress, instead of starting with a canned sales presentation.

What do our prospects feel when we read their minds?

Connection. Rapport. Trust. And because we know exactly what they want, we avoid objections and procrastination. How good is that?

Amateur marketers waste hours with rapport-building conversations and presentations. They present business propositions or products that their prospects don't want. It is this disconnect that makes sales impossible. It is like we are in two different conversations. We are not listening to their conversation, and they are not listening to ours.

Professional marketers understand their prospects, what their prospects want, and their buying motives. They know what their prospects want to achieve, and of course, offer to help them get it.

Plus, professional marketers use mind reading to build that strong connection and trust so that "yes" decisions are easy. They don't have to deal with objections, because objections won't happen. Their customized messages bypass the natural objections prospects might have.

Mind reading isn't only about understanding what our prospects want, but more importantly about how they feel. Taking this extra step is important. Why? Because decisions are made by emotions, not facts. Our prospects are human. They have many emotions and subconscious programs controlling their actions.

Get ready for a fun journey into our prospects' minds. Our mind-reading superpowers will give us instant empathy and results. And before we doubt our ability to learn these superpowers, a quick reminder. We do mind reading now. We just didn't know it. We will discover our hidden talent in the chapters ahead.

And finally, let's not forget the big picture.

"The only thing between us, and where we want to be, is ... a bunch of stuff we don't know yet. Because if we knew the stuff, we would be there already!"

Let's learn new stuff every day.

THE SCARIEST THING I EVER DID?

I am not brave. Sweating and tense, I enter the "Valley of Dark Creepy Things."

Yes, I walk into an automobile dealership to attempt to buy a car. As I enter the front door, the lights dim. Sunlight disappears. Suddenly a deep fog engulfs the room. And from the ceiling, drops a vampire salesperson, blood dripping from his fangs from his last car sale.

"Can I help you?" Huh? This was a strange way to trick me.

"I want to uh, uh, uh, to buy a car. I want a bargain. Quote me your best deal." I didn't sound brave.

Bad positioning by me already. Cringe. I adjust my garlic protective necklace. My fear paralyzes me from running away.

The vampire salesperson drools, leans back, and politely asks, "What kind of car interests you? Are you looking for something flashy to impress people, or something practical that saves money? And how long do you plan to keep this car as I am sure you want to consider the resale value?"

Huh? What???? I am shocked! A non-sleazy vampire car salesperson? Someone who cares and asks questions? What kind of nightmare is this?

I panic. "Uh, uh. I'm just looking. I am not even interested. I walked in here by mistake. I thought it was a donut shop."

The vampire salesperson grins. With piercing eyes and a slow, deep voice, he calmly says, "Look into my eyes."

Oh no! I'm not falling for this. I know what comes next. I watch all the vampire movies.

He continues. "Relax. Look deeply into my eyes. You are brave for coming in here alone. I don't have to sell you a car because you already know you need to get a car. However, I can help you choose the right car, so you make the best choice for your family."

My feet felt glued to the ground. I relaxed.

This vampire car salesperson read my mind!

That is exactly what I was hoping for. And with a sigh of relief, I think, "I like this vampire. He reads my mind. He understands what I need and is here to help me. Maybe buying a car won't be so bad after all."

If a mind-reading vampire car salesperson can overcome a prospect's fear and skepticism ... and sell a car, then, so can we.

Mind reading superpowers create immediate trust and connection. This is the secret ingredient of superstars.

So let's leave the vampires behind, and enter the world of human prospects. Let's learn how to turn on our mind reading superpowers.

WHERE IT ALL GOES WRONG

We make offers to our prospects ... and then things go terribly wrong.

Rejection. Skepticism. Bias. Prejudice. Folded arms. We get ghosted. Objections, and more. So what is wrong?

We know exactly what we say. But, do we know what our prospects hear?

What if this was the conversation inside our prospects' heads?

"Oh no. Another salesperson. Don't believe a word this salesperson says. Salespeople will tell us anything, including lies, just to get us to buy."

Whoa! This certainly is not what we want our prospects to think.

Sure, it feels bad that we are being judged like this, but let's think about our prospects. This is a real disservice to our prospects.

We could have the perfect offer to solve our prospects' problems. But if they are skeptical, and don't believe a word we say, they won't take this opportunity to improve their lives. We effectively withhold our wonderful offer because we can't break through their skepticism.

Now, is that what we want? Is that what our prospects want? Of course not.

We want our prospects to judge our offer on our offer's merits, and not let silly mind programs cloud our message or prejudice our prospects' minds.

Our message must be clear.

Our message must be heard.

Only then our prospects can make an intelligent decision if our offer can serve them or not. That is our goal.

SOUNDS GOOD, BUT IS THIS POSSIBLE?

Yes. The secret is to create a strong rapport with our prospects.

Rapport? What do we mean by rapport?

In selling, the most important skill is the ability to build rapport with our prospects. Personality, salespersonship skills, enthusiasm, and everything else come in second place.

Rapport means this:

- A relationship
- Agreement
- Trust
- Belief
- Understanding
- Get along
- Harmony
- Close connection
- Cooperation
- Empathy
- We think the same way
- Friendly

- We see the world from the same viewpoint
- Joined-at-the-hip
- Vulcan mind-meld
- Blood brother or blood sister

Okay, we get the idea. When we have a strong rapport with our prospects, they will listen to us and hear what we have to offer. Simple.

What are some common ways we use to connect with people and build rapport?

- Use their name in conversation
- Everyone loves a good listener
- Use NLP or try to match and mirror their body language
- Look for common past experiences
- Ask open-ended questions
- Nod and look into their eyes while listening
- And, avoid telling them they are stupid. Obvious

These methods work well when we use them correctly and with good intentions. However, there is another powerful way to create rapport with our prospects. This method is called … mind reading.

When we understand what is on our prospects' minds, they think,

"I can trust this person. I can trust what this person says. I can believe the message. This person understands me and how I see the world."

And that is all we ask.

If our prospects receive our message clearly, they can decide if our message will serve them or not. And since we won't waste our time with bad or non-serving messages, most prospects will want to do business with us.

By mastering mind reading at a higher level, we can say good-bye to objections, resistance, bias, and prejudice. Instead, let's welcome stress-free conversations with prospects who love us.

But … we want to do this at a higher level, right?

We are not going to settle for ordinary rapport-building methods. Let's preview where we are going with our soon-to-be-mastered mind reading superpowers. Here is a personal case study.

RECOVERING FROM STUPIDITY

I was in a bit of a rush, and didn't build a good rapport. Now, it was costing me. My prospects were hesitating and didn't want to join. This was all my fault.

I knew the business was great for them. They needed the extra money, were well-respected, and had many friends who would be eager to buy from them. Seemed perfect, but there was a gap in the connection between them and me. So they hesitated.

I had to build a deeper connection fast. To do this, I thought back in our conversation to look for the possible objection, the hidden reason that kept them from moving forward.

They were proud of their reputation, and that was the clue I needed. They secretly worried about what others would think if they joined a network marketing business.

Time to put mind reading into action.

Before I show you what I said, let me help with a little sneak preview of a magic mind reading phrase that we will be learning in upcoming chapters. Ready?

- "I find that most people ..."

Let's break down this phrase.

"I find that ..." This phrase causes prospects to think, "Okay, you are reporting what you observed. What fact, truth or event did you notice?" Now, what we say next won't sound like a sales pitch. Just a report.

"Most people." This phrase causes prospects to think, "Most people, eh? Let me think. Am I part of most people, or am I part of less people? I guess I am part of most people. I tend to do what most people do. I think like most people. Yeah, I am a most people type of person."

Watch for these two phrases as I continue to talk to my hesitating prospects. Ready?

"I find that most people worry about what their friends will think if they start their own part-time business. This is natural because we live in our community 100% of the time. But the good news is that **most people** have great friends who are happy that we are improving our lives and want to support and help us. I guess we inspire them."

The couple looked at each other. I could feel our connection get stronger. They wanted to be like most people who have great friends. They felt that I not only read their minds about what was bothering them, but that I also had empathy. I understood the emotions they were feeling.

This moment changed everything.

The objection was gone.

The hesitation was gone.

And you might be wondering, "Why I didn't do this simple mind reading connection earlier?"

Because I needed more of these embarrassing lessons before I learned the habit to create strong rapport before I continue my conversations. Slow learner here.

MIND READING
IS EMPATHY
ON STEROIDS

Yes, mind reading qualifies as a superpower. It is the ultimate expression of empathy. When we see life from our prospects' point of view, selling and communication is easy. This is like putting on x-ray glasses and knowing what our prospects feel.

This is what is wrong with most sales presentations. Salespeople present what they think is important. They bore prospects with videos, brochures, weak testimonials, company background, and endless lists, features, and specifications. Ugh!

Their prospects feel that something else is important, and become impatient with the salesperson. Two different conversations happening, and no one is connecting.

What happens? Stress, frustration, folded arms, skepticism, and prospects who want to leave. In the worst cases, prospects will harbor thoughts of violence. Okay, maybe not that bad, but some pushy salespeople do push the limits.

The secret is to focus on our prospects, not ourselves. It is not about us, it is all about them. When we can do this, everything else falls into place.

AMATEUR SALESPEOPLE ARE THE WORST

Our advice to new salespeople? The first step is to get rid of their sales presentation. Trash it. Our prospects don't care about us or our product. They only care about themselves and their problems. Yes, prospects are selfish that way.

What does our ordinary, boring, self-centered sales presentation look like? Here is an exaggerated summary.

- Listen to me
- My company is great
- Let me tell you why my company is great
- Watch my wonderful video commercial
- Here are all the things my company does
- We do all these things better than everyone else
- Let me tell you about all the things my company offers
- Look at this data that proves my company is great
- This is what my product looks like
- This is how my product works
- Read these testimonials from happy customers
- Let me tell you about the features of my product
- Here are the specifications of my product
- Buy my product now and you will get an extra bonus
- You need my product
- Trust me, I am a salesperson
- I have been in sales for years
- You can't live without my product
- Listen to my power close

Wow. No wonder prospects don't want to buy. They never get to say a word.

If the purpose of business is to solve our prospects' problems, how will we ever know what their problems are if we never let them talk?

Selling isn't about talking. Selling is listening to prospects to find out what they think. This is what makes mind reading so easy. If we are good listeners, our prospects will tell us exactly what they think! We don't even have to be good at this. Just take notes!

But, we will get even better over time. With experience, we will know what most prospects think. Then, with a few chosen phrases, our prospects will feel a deep connection as if we are reading their minds.

Sound like a plan?

Let's start with a simple case study of salespeople who didn't listen. Plus, in this case study, we will learn some key strategies that we can use immediately. Ready?

CLUELESS AND HOPELESS

Ten years ago, while doing a workshop tour in England, one of the attendees asked me, "Could I ask a favor?"

"Uh … well … sure, go ahead and ask."

He stutters and said, "I am a personal trainer at our local gym. My fellow personal trainers and I get paid on commission, and we are having trouble closing prospects. No one wants to sign up for our workout plan. Could you come by our gym tonight and talk to us? Please? We need help. You are an expert."

I am thinking, "Expert? I can only do 11% of a pushup! I can't even do heavy breathing exercises. But I do know a tip or two that would help them close prospects."

So of course, I agreed and went to their gym that night. It was a packed room of motivated, broke, frustrated, and incredibly fit personal trainers. These personal trainers were fired up.

I started by asking the group, "What do you say now to close the deal?" Their answers made me cringe.

Take a deep breath before reading their closing sentences. They said:

- "How did you like your free workout?"
- "Uh, uh, want to sign up and give us money?"
- "I know this workout hurt, but sign up now so you can feel this way again."

- "I hate to see you leave, but if you must, can I interest you in our other services like tanning?"
- "We have a great deal for you if you sign up today before you leave."
- "So, what do you think? Are you ready to make a commitment?"
- "Why don't you stop crying about how bad this hurts, and just sign up for more sessions?"

My thoughts?

Any closing statement that I would give this group would be better than what they are saying now. I wouldn't have to be very good at this to look like a superstar. No competition from the personal trainers. Their ideas could be summarized by this one eager attendee.

One personal trainer, who looked under-aged, stepped up to the front of the room. He said, "This is my strategy. If my prospect doesn't want to hire me, I keep pestering him until he agrees."

Instant applause. High fives. I could see the personal trainers getting excited. They felt inspired to go out to nag and harass their prospects. More muscle flexing.

Groan. There was work to do here.

There were so many things wrong with what they did, that I hardly knew where to start. Let's begin with the obvious.

PROBLEM #1: THE PERSONAL TRAINERS HAD A TERRIBLE WORKOUT STRATEGY

In the free trial workout, the personal trainers wanted to prove how awesome they were, and how weak the prospects were. They ground the prospects down through a grueling workout session to prove how much the prospects needed their services. And then, while the prospect was writhing in pain, their closing question was, "Do you want more of this pain? Come on. Sign up for more, please?"

No empathy here.

The personal trainers seemed okay with torturing their prospects.

Let's look at this from the prospect's perspective. They come to the gym, but they are not sure if they want to sign up for a personal trainer. They see other people in great shape, and they think, "I want to be like them." So, they try a free workout. The personal trainer smiles, but the prospects don't realize that this is an evil smile from their soon-to-be torturer.

The workout is intense. The prospects are not used to working out this hard. They are huffing and puffing. They feel death is imminent. Black spots appear before their eyes. Hearing loss begins. Now they feel concerned. And then, when they are at their most painful levels, the personal trainer asks them if they want to sign up for more pain.

Gee, what could possibly go wrong with this strategy?

Q. So, what would be a better strategy?

A. Anything else!

How about making the introductory workout a bit more tolerable? If prospects felt better when they finished, wouldn't selling a personal trainer contract be easier?

The personal trainers looked puzzled. Why? Because they only thought about themselves. They failed to have empathy for their prospects. I am thinking, "Do big muscles reduce brain size? Don't they think their services would be easier to sell if people enjoyed their services?"

Slowly, a few personal trainers begin to nod in agreement. Closing would be easier if their prospects wanted to continue the experience. Progress.

PROBLEM #2: THE PERSONAL TRAINERS HAD NO UNDERSTANDING OF BASIC HUMAN BRAIN PSYCHOLOGY

Human brains aren't complicated.

First, our brains are programmed for survival. Our brains' #1 priority is to keep us alive, to avoid dangerous situations such as heaving massive amounts of weight above our heads. Looks like the personal trainers violated this priority.

Second, our brains like easy over hard, pleasure over pain, and simple over complicated. These are easy choices to make. Easy choices don't consume much brain power. When faced with an easy solution over a hard solution, our brains can figure this out in less than a second. No rocket science neurons are required. Our brains look at these choices as options. And of course, we want to pick the better option.

The personal trainers made everything complicated. Their sales process, their confusing pricing, their contracts, and most importantly, their close. They gave their prospects too many options. ("Do you want to sign up for 1 month, 3 months, 6 months, or 12 months with bonus points?")

What do human brains prefer for choices? Only two choices.

We don't want to waste precious brainpower to juggle four or seven choices simultaneously in our working memory space.

Doesn't work. We want two options: good or bad, easy or hard, black or white, or yes or no.

Let's start our brain science lesson here.

"OUR BRAINS LIKE EASY OVER HARD, PLEASURE OVER PAIN, SIMPLE OVER COMPLICATED"

"Easy over hard"

Let's put ourselves into our prospects' minds. They're asking themselves, "Do I want to get in shape the hard way, or the easy way?" Their answer is obvious. They want the easy way.

What could our personal trainers say to signal to their prospects that having a personal trainer is the "easy way" to get fit? How about something like this?

"You can get in shape on your own. It's not easy. It's hard work. You have to be self-motivated, disciplined, and have a lot of willpower. Plus, most of your exercises will be wasted. You will spend twice as much time getting results. Or, you can make it easy on yourself and hire me as your personal trainer. I'll make sure every exercise creates the maximum results so that you don't have to waste hours every day getting nowhere. All you have to do is show up."

Did we notice that the personal trainers now offer only two options? Option #1: the hard way. Option #2: the easy way.

Progress.

"Pleasure over pain"

Again, let's put ourselves into our prospects' minds. They're asking themselves, "Do I want my journey to get in shape to be pleasurable or painful?"

Once again, the answer is obvious. Human brains vote for pleasure.

How can our personal trainers change their closing words to make them more pleasurable for their prospects?

Let's try a couple of ideas.

"You can work out on your own, but it will be more painful. The wrong exercises, at the wrong time, can cause serious injuries. There is nothing worse than suffering and tolerating painful injuries week after week. Or ... you can use my expertise to guide you through safe exercises that feel good and are fun to do."

How about another example?

"You can do random exercises on your own, and make this gym look like a torture chamber to your mind. Or, you can let me guide you through efficient workouts that make you feel great. You will look forward to coming to the gym."

Again, only two choices.

Our prospects will choose pleasure over pain almost every time.

"Simple versus complicated"

The personal trainers complicated the close by giving their prospects too many options. This is the exact opposite of what our brains want. We want simple, not complicated. What happens when we have too many choices? We can't make a decision.

But it gets worse. If we have too many choices, we won't have room in our brains for the important things in life, such as scrolling for sarcastic or humorous social media posts. Just kidding. Okay, maybe not. Our brains get a dopamine hit from scrolling. We like that. But, back to the point.

Remember the personal trainer's original options? "Do you want to sign up for 1 month, 3 months, 6 months, or 12 months with bonus points?" Too complicated. Our brains don't want to waste time trying to figure out the best deal.

We want a simple choice.

Let's try a few ideas.

"You can try to get in shape on your own, but it's complicated. You have to figure out what exercises to do, how often to do them, when to do them, and how to stay motivated. It's a lot of work. Or ... you can make it simple and hire me as your personal trainer so that you can enjoy your results fast."

"You can stay out of shape forever. That is a choice. Or, you can sign up for a 1-month membership and see how you feel in 30 days. If you like the results, then you can sign up for a longer term."

Only two choices. And they are simple choices.

Our prospects can make a decision without having to think too much.

How about a bonus choice for human brains?

"Certain over uncertain."

Which feels better to our human brains? Certainty or uncertainty? The answer is obvious. Uncertainty gives us stress. We hate to worry about an unknown future.

How can our personal trainers change their close to make it more certain for their prospects?

Let's try a quick example.

"You can work out and hope to get in shape on your own, but it's uncertain. You don't know if you're doing the right exercises, or if you're doing them correctly, or if those exercises will even make a difference. You could end up wasting months or years without seeing any results. Or, you can hire me as your personal trainer as I will make sure every exercise you do gets you in shape faster."

Only two choices.

Waste time and money with no results, or get certain results with a personal trainer.

The choice is clear.

PROBLEM #3: FEATURES, BENEFITS, AND THE BENEFIT OF THE BENEFIT

When our personal trainers attempted to close their prospects, they focused on the features of their services.

- "1-hour sessions, twice a week."
- "Small group classes."
- "Expertise in weight loss."
- "Alternate muscle group training."
- "Shiny new bench press recently polished."
- "Instructors with multiple certificates of completion."

Yawn. The personal trainers were lucky that their prospects didn't fall asleep, especially after the grueling workout. No one cares about our features.

Humans care about benefits.

What's the difference between features and benefits?

A feature is a fact about our product or service. A benefit is what that feature does for our prospects. Let's do some examples.

"1-hour sessions, twice a week." This is a feature of their services. But what's the benefit?

The benefit might be that it only takes one hour, and the prospect could do it over an extended lunch. Now our prospect wouldn't have to wake up at 5 a.m. in the morning for his or her workout. This could be a huge benefit for someone who is not a morning person.

"Shiny new bench press recently polished." This is a stupid feature. How could we make it better? Let's revise this feature. "Our bench press is always clean because we have magical elves wipe the sweat off our bench presses after every use." Hmmm. What is the benefit of having these hard-working elves? "We won't smell like other people's sweat after using the bench press."

Think of benefits as the reason we want particular features.

But, we can get better!

"What is the benefit of the benefit?"

Now we are digging deeper into what our prospects want. An easy way to understand this is to continue the questioning, "Why is this benefit important to my prospect?"

Taking that extra step feels like mind reading. Our prospects will think, "Wow. You understand me. You think like me. You are probably a genius just like me. I can trust you and believe you. Just tell me what to do."

Let's use this "benefit of the benefit" technique on our two feature/benefit examples. Ready?

Feature: "1-hour sessions, twice a week."

Benefit: "You can do this during lunch, so you don't have to get up at 5 am."

Benefit of the benefit: "You will be in shape and can show off your new body to your flabby co-workers who stayed behind and make them feel jealous."

Feature: "Shiny new bench press recently polished."

Benefit: "The benchpress is always clean. You won't smell like other people's sweat."

Benefit of the benefit: "You will be proud to work out in our gym because it is so clean and other gyms are so gross. Plus your pit bull won't attack you when you get home because you smell like a stranger's sweat. And as an added bonus, you can tell your friends that you work out at the only gym that employs full-time magical elves. What a great conversation starter."

CLOSING ISN'T SCARY

Take a look at the ideas and choices we offered so far. Now, let's compare these with the original closing statements our personal trainers used.

- "How did you like your free workout?"
- "Uh, uh, want to sign up and give us money?"
- "I know this workout hurt, but sign up now so you can feel this way again."
- "I hate to see you leave, but if you must, can I interest you in our other services like tanning?"

- "We have a great deal for you if you sign up today before you leave."

- "So, what do you think? Are you ready to make a commitment?"

- "Why don't you stop crying about how bad this hurts, and just sign up for more sessions?"

The difference between an amateur, and a real professional, is ... success!

BUT ... BUT ... HOW WILL WE MAKE THIS HAPPEN?

Okay, the personal trainers gave us a lesson in how bad we can be. And, we learned how to talk to and close prospects better. That case study seemed to be something about empathy? Mind reading? Connection? Brain rules?

Something was working, and we want to learn how to do it. Let's start here.

HOW CAN WE SIGNAL TO OUR PROSPECTS THAT WE CAN READ THEIR MINDS, AND UNDERSTAND THEIR FEARS?

With the words we say.

We can use simple phrases and sentences that put our prospects at ease. Now our message gets through.

Are these mind reading phrases difficult? No.

Do we have to have some sort of psychic powers? No.

Do we need superhuman skills? No.

Do we need the power of a trained mentalist? No.

Certain phrases and sentences will signal to our prospects that we know the concerns in their minds, and ... have it all under control. Basic salespersonship, a bit of human psychology, and a dose of persuasion skills are all we will need.

When we use these skills, our prospects feel a high-level connection and will trust us.

WHERE DO WE START?

Here are common thoughts in most prospects' minds:

- "I'm afraid of making the wrong decision."
- "I don't want to be taken advantage of."
- "I am afraid of change."
- "Can I trust you?"
- "I'm not sure if I believe you."
- "I need to know that you understand my situation."
- "What will others think?"
- "Is there some sort of guarantee?"
- "Have others tried this first?
- "I'm not sure if I can afford this."
- "I need to think about it."
- "I am afraid to make decisions."

Whew! That is a lot of internal dialogue. Plenty of choices for us. Need more?

- "I'm afraid I might fail."
- "I don't understand everything."
- "I don't have time for this."
- "I need more information."
- "I'm not sure if this is right for me."

- "Is there someone else I can talk to about this?"
- "I'm just not ready."
- "No one has ever helped me before."
- "I'm afraid to take the first step."
- "I don't want to be disappointed."
- "How do I know this will work for me?"
- "I'm afraid I'll be let down."
- "I'm not sure if this is what I really want."

These are only a few of the many issues our prospects have running through their minds. Most prospects are thinking these thoughts while we are speaking.

Wait!

If most prospects are thinking these thoughts while we are speaking, that means they won't be listening to us!

Oh.

So … instead of talking about us and our stuff, let's enter our prospects' minds, and join their internal conversation.

And guess what? Now we have an audience for our words.

By adding a few simple phrases, we will appear to have super-human mind reading powers. Our prospects will be impressed.

Let's start now with the most simple phrase.

LET'S START WITH SOME SAFE WORDS

Nervous about reading other people's minds? Afraid that we might guess wrong? That would be embarrassing.

Well, guess what? We just guessed what was on our minds. Of course, we worry we might make a mistake. But how hard was this to guess? Most people have the same thoughts and worries as we do.

So if we don't feel confident in our mind reading ability, we don't have to make a win/lose guess. Instead, we can just make a statement of what "most people" would be thinking. Totally safe. No risk. We are just commenting on what "most people" would be thinking.

Chances are that our prospects will fall into the category of "most people" so this will appear as if we are reading their minds. Now, what words will make this easy and automatic for us? Let's use these words, "most people." Some examples?

- I find that most people worry about the future.
- I find that most people are careful about spending their own money.
- I find that most people find making decisions a bit scary.
- I find that most people are hesitant to try something new.

- I find that most people are skeptical about new ideas.

- I find that most people want to know more before they make up their minds.

Now, let's combine several of these phrases to introduce our products or services in a way that feels as if we are reading our prospects' minds. Ready?

For investment services we could say:

"Most people worry about the future. They wonder if they will have enough money to retire. They are careful about spending their own money. That's why our investment services make sense. We can help you plan for a comfortable retirement."

For our business opportunity we could say:

"Most people worry about the future. They wonder if they will have enough money to retire. They are careful about spending their own money. That's why our part-time business opportunity makes sense."

This feels easy.

We are not guessing what is in our prospects' minds. We are simply making statements about what "most people" think. Our chances are good that our prospects will identify with these thoughts. So, we appear to be reading their minds.

Because we did this, our prospects can relax. They think, "This person understands me. This person reads my mind. I can trust that this person will see the world from the same viewpoint as I do."

Seems easy, doesn't it?

Most of us are not born mind readers. (This was a mind-reading phrase. Feel it?)

We can use these "most people" phrases as a way to establish rapport and trust with our prospects.

How difficult is this? Just two words, "Most people."

That didn't take long to learn. And, this is a skill that we can use immediately.

IS THIS HARD-WIRED INTO OUR BRAINS?

Yes. Everyone has a survival program. Our survival program tells us this, "I want to survive. I want to feel safe. Let me stay with the group, and not be a loner. Life is safer when I am in a group. I want to be like everyone else in the group."

It feels safe when we hear someone say, "Most people think this way."

Humans naturally think in terms of "most people." This is a no-brainer. Totally safe.

Now, let's look at a few "most people" phrases that move us closer to new customers and new team members.

- I find that most people like to know how to get started.
- I find that most people naturally think, "Can I do this?"
- I find that most people think this makes sense.
- I find that most people don't want to fall behind.
- I find that most people are afraid of making the wrong decision.
- I find that most people want to save money.
- I find that most people think, "How can I take advantage of this?"

- I find that most people worry when they make changes in their lives.

- I find that most people are hesitant to try something new.

- I find that most people are skeptical about new ideas.

- I find that most people have a question or two. What can I answer for you?"

Notice how these mind-reading phrases establish rapport and trust?

Let's combine a few of these phrases for some fun. Ready?

"It is okay to worry. Most people worry when they make changes in their lives. That's natural. But, most people also like to know how to get started as they think this makes sense."

It doesn't take much imagination to see how a few chosen words can change how our prospects feel about us.

These rapport-building phrases let our prospects know that we understand them and we are like them. And since we are like them, they can accept our clear message without resistance.

But we are just starting. Let's learn more little phrases that will make our prospects feel great.

HEAVY-METAL VERSUS BLUEGRASS MUSIC

Rapport. The feeling that we have a connection with the other person. We see the world in the same way.

What happens if we don't see the world in the same way? Distrust. Skepticism. Doubt.

We need rapport to deliver our offer or message in a way that our prospects will "hear us" without prejudice or bias. Remember. That is all we ask. We want our message to be clear and heard by our prospects.

But what happens if we don't connect? Let's see.

BAD MUSIC

Our bluegrass music fan accidentally books a ticket to a heavy metal concert. "Oh well, I paid for the ticket. No refunds. I might as well go."

What happens? Our bluegrass music fan's eardrums explode. He can't understand the lyrics. Breathing is difficult as the air is filled with a funny-smelling smoke.

Surrounded by metalheads and headbangers, how do you think our bluegrass music fan feels? Comfortable? Trusting?

Connected? We won't hear our bluegrass music friend yell, "I should get a season ticket!"

This is a mismatch. No rapport. No connection.

The same thing happens when we don't read the minds of our prospects. If we don't understand how they see the world, we can't speak their language.

What would happen if a heavy metal fan attends a bluegrass music festival? Well, it wouldn't be so traumatic. But a bonding experience? Not a chance. Our heavy metal fan cringes when he hears the first banjo twang. He won't stomp his foot in time with the bluegrass music.

What would be the response if the bluegrass music fans recommend guitar brands to our heavy metal fan? Their message would fall on deaf ears. No rapport. No connection. No sale.

PERCEPTION

Perceptions are more important than facts. People are more likely to listen to what we have to say if they believe we understand them. If they don't perceive us as someone who understands them, they will tune us out. Simple.

Empathy is the ability to understand the feelings of another. If we can't empathize with our prospects, we won't be able to read their minds. And if we can't read their minds, we won't be able to connect with them.

Here's an example.

A salesperson is trying to sell a car to a potential customer. The salesperson doesn't ask questions or listens. He doesn't know that the potential customer lost his job last week. He is worried about making ends meet. The last thing he wants to do is spend money on an expensive car.

What happens? The salesperson keeps talking about the features of a more expensive car. The wonderful presentation falls on deaf ears. The customer tunes him out. No connection. No sale.

But what if we listen? What if our prospects tell us their concerns?

Which words or phrases can we use to signal to our prospects that we understand them? What can we say that makes our prospects feel as if we are reading their minds, seeing the world through their viewpoint? Look at what our salesperson should have said.

"I know you're concerned about your budget right now, so let me show you how this car fits your budget."

The salesperson connects with the prospect.

How? With these two words.

"I KNOW ..."

That was simple. These two words tell our prospects we read their minds, and understand what they are feeling. Remember, feelings are emotions, and emotions trigger action. Ready for some examples?

- I know how important it is to be able to trust the person you are doing business with.
- I know it is hard to believe we don't have to work 45 years of hard labor before retirement.
- I know you want to get the most for your money.
- I know you want to be careful with your money.
- I know you worry about how expensive this problem is.

- I know you are afraid of making the wrong decision.
- I know you are concerned about how much time this will take.
- I know you want more options in your life.
- I know you want to fix this problem.
- I know you are considering other options, but this option will get results faster.
- I know you are trying to decide what will be best for you.
- I know you are curious about how others did this.

The words "I know" signal to our prospects that we understand them. We see the world through their eyes. They can hear us without prejudice or bias.

Just be careful not to overuse "I know" when talking to our prospects.

With this simple phrase, our prospects feel better. They see that we have empathy and understand what they feel. Again, since most people have these same thoughts, it is easy to appear that we are mind reading.

Empathy. The ability to understand and share the feelings of others. Seeing the world through their eyes, and putting ourselves in their shoes. This is a great feeling for our prospects that they are talking with someone with empathy.

What do our prospects want more than anything else?

The answer is simple. They want to be understood. Our prospects want to feel valued, important, and special. They want to be seen as an individual, not as a faceless prospect. they want a connection with us. This is what we must signal to them through our words and actions

Here is the good news. Because prospects want to talk with someone who has empathy, we don't have to be 100% accurate. They are okay if they perceive that we are at least trying to understand their feelings.

This is why hard-core salespeople have difficulties. They believe in one-way communication, talking AT their prospects. These hard-core salespeople are so busy with their facts, features, benefits, PowerPoint presentations, and controlling the conversation, they miss the big picture. Prospects prefer to do business with people they know, like, and trust.

Let's add a few more "I know" mind reading phrases to our mental libraries. Ready?

- I know you're wondering how this could work.
- I know you're trying to figure out if you need this or not.
- I know you are skeptical about this.
- I know you think this is too good to be true.
- I know you want to see what others think also.
- I know you wish you could predict the future.
- I know you want guaranteed results.
- I know you want to make sure this is the right decision.
- I know it is scary when making a big change.
- I know you want to weigh all of your options first.
- I know you feel like you are taking a risk, but you do want this to pay off.
- I know that trusting someone new can be difficult.
- I know you are concerned about this.
- I know this is a lot to think about.

- I know you want to make the right decision.
- I know you want what is best for the family.

This is natural sales language that doesn't trigger the salesperson's alarm. We all have said these phrases before:

- I know how you feel,
- I know what you were thinking.
- I know you don't want to take any chances.

Sound familiar? "I know" is a safe mind reading phrase. We don't need any training on this. Simple and effective.

Safe mind reading makes sense now. If we have empathy, this will feel natural. All we need to do is to place simple phrases in front of common facts that signal that we are "reading their minds."

STILL HESITANT?

Want to make this "I know" statement completely risk-free? Try this version of the "I know" phrase:

"I feel like you are …"

Who can argue with how we feel? Only we know how we feel. 100% safe. Here are a few examples.

- I feel like you are worried about the investment.
- I feel like you want to be safe and never take a risk.
- I feel like you want to know more, just to be sure.
- I feel like you are worried that you might be scammed.
- I feel like you are worried if this will affect your job.

We stated our feelings, but it shows that we have empathy. When our prospects hear our feelings, and our feelings are accurate, they are impressed.

What do we feel right now? (Yes, another mind reading is coming.)

We feel like we want to know more simple phrases that signal we have high-level mind reading powers.

I KNOW YOU ARE THINKING THIS.

What are some more safe "I know" statements that we can say that are under the radar, that won't trigger prospects to feel skepticism or manipulation? Let's try these.

- I know you're extremely busy and don't have time to waste.
- I know you have been thinking about a way to solve this problem.
- I know you want to find a solution that can work.
- I know you wonder what is the best way to solve this problem.
- I know you don't want to make the wrong decision.
- I know you are looking for a solution that fits your budget.
- I know you worry that you will have enough time.
- I know you worry about getting scammed.
- I know you worry if this will affect your job.
- I know this phone call is an interruption.
- I know how important it is to be able to trust the person you're working with.

And (I can't resist) …

- I know you worry about how you will explain this to your spouse.

Let's think about this from our prospects' point of view. Imagine we say, "I know you want to be careful."

What thoughts do we trigger in our prospects' minds? Their minds react by thinking, "Great! This salesperson understands me. This salesperson won't be high-pressuring me for a quick decision."

With this fear out of the way, prospects can listen to our offer without filters and prejudice. Now they will hear our clear message.

But, this connection can get even better.

FEAR

It is a dark and scary night. As we walk through the cemetery, we hear the faint sound of heavy breathing behind us. We look. No one is there. And then we feel a coldness across our sweating foreheads. We know we are being watched. Or, is someone stalking us? Or something?

More chills down our spine. Our heart races. We start to run. But, we can't shake the feeling that someone or something is following us. And then ...

We feel a boney hand grip our throats. Another hand covers our eyes. Fear paralyzes our bodies. We smell the stench of death. We know we are going to die.

As we struggle to survive, we push a finger away from our eyes and see our attacker ...

A salesperson!

"Hi, I'm Joe Salesperson. I saw you walking alone and thought you would want to purchase our new stress tablets. These scientific wonders are thoroughly tested, copyrighted, trademarked, and patented. Our scientists can beat up the competition's scientists. These tablets can withstand ..."

FEAR IS REAL

Everyone has fear. Fear of the unknown. Fear of change. Fear of rejection. Fear of the judgment of others. Fear of looking stupid. Fear of making decisions. Fear of pushy salespeople.

Everyone has fear. Okay, almost everyone. A few outliers with no fear are busy performing death-defying circus acts for a living. We don't get many of these outliers as our prospects.

Fear is natural. Amateur salespeople hope to find people who don't have the fear of making decisions. A delusional goal? Yes.

Instead of searching for mythical prospects who have no fear of making decisions, professional salespeople spend their time learning skills to lower the fear levels in their prospects.

Will we ever make the fear of the unknown, or the fear of the future go away? No. But we can help our prospects manage that fear, so they are no longer paralyzed and will move ahead.

Mind reading is the skill that will help us lower the fear levels in our prospects. Our mind reading tells our prospects, "You are not alone. I understand. I am here with you."

There is safety in numbers. That scary cemetery walk at night feels better if we have a companion.

THE WORDS

What words communicate to our prospects that we understand and empathize with their fears? Let's try these.

- It is natural to feel that way.
- It is natural to fear change.
- It is natural to worry about what others will think.

- It is natural to feel anxiety when making decisions.
- It is natural to stress and overthink big financial decisions.
- It is natural to be cautious when trying something new.
- It is natural to put off maintenance until it is too late.
- It is natural to avoid thinking about this problem.
- It is natural to wish this would go away.
- It is natural to wish problems fixed themselves.
- It is natural to want to avoid talking about this problem.
- It is natural to want to delay decisions, and hope our decisions get made for us.

Our prospects' reactions? They think, "Wow. This is natural. I don't have to feel embarrassed that I am hesitating. Other people think like me."

It is natural for professional marketers to use this pattern. We start by saying, "It is natural ...", and our prospects feel we understand their fears.

Need a few more?

- It's natural to be a little uncertain about something new.
- It's natural to be cautious when starting a new venture.
- It's natural to feel hesitant about big purchases.
- It's natural to feel shy when meeting someone new.
- It's natural to be a little apprehensive.
- It's natural to be a little skeptical about making a first-time purchase like this.
- It's natural to be a little shy at first. I completely understand.

Okay, we got the pattern.

If we don't feel good about the "it's natural" phrasing, try using "it's normal." We want to feel natural when we do this.

HOW CAN OUR PROSPECTS TURN DOWN OUR WONDERFUL OFFER?

Think about our wonderful offers. What we offer is an improvement in our prospects' lives.

Logically, we win every time.

Emotionally, we lose every time, unless we take action to help our prospects overcome their fears.

Fear is an emotion. Emotions crush silly logical reasons. Trying to get our prospects to agree that our logical offer makes sense is a waste of time. The critical issue is not the value we offer, but the ability to overcome the "fear of change" emotion. Let's focus on what is important, their fear of change.

It is natural for us to want more word patterns to address these fears. Ready?

"I UNDERSTAND"

Our prospects hesitate. We say these words, "I understand." What do our prospects feel?

They think, "I don't have to argue with you. I don't have to explain what I am going through. You understand me. I don't have to come up with more creative negative excuses."

This is a better conversation in our prospects' heads than, "Oh no! A salesperson. Now I have to look for reasons to resist, and reasons to protect myself from a high-pressure close."

Yes, we want to be on the same side as our prospects. Let's try a few "I understand" statements now.

- I understand why you may be hesitant.
- I understand why you want to ask more questions.
- I understand that you want to find the best option possible.
- I understand why committing is hard.
- I understand what it is like to be in your position. I was there myself.
- I understand why we wish the future was guaranteed.
- I understand why are you worried that this could be too expensive.
- I understand that we worry about what others think of us.

Of course, we won't say all of these things when we talk to our prospects. But, we should find one or two versions that feel comfortable for us.

But, what if we think that saying "I understand" is too risky? Maybe it might feel too presumptuous at times. In that case, let's soften this phrase by saying, "I can understand ..." It is hard for someone to challenge or argue about what is happening in our minds.

Some quick examples.

- I can understand why we might be shy about asking more questions.
- I can understand why you might be feeling this way.
- I can understand how this would be a big concern for you.
- I can understand why you might want to put off purchasing as long as you can.

- I can understand why you might want to wait.

- I can understand why you worry about how others feel about your decisions.

- I can understand why we hesitate, but also fear that we might be left behind.

"FEAR THAT WE MIGHT BE LEFT BEHIND?"

Yes, that is a real fear. No one wants to be using a rotary telephone from the 1960s in a smartphone world. The fear of being left behind can be the reason to make a decision to move forward now. We should keep this in mind when talking to hesitant prospects. Which fear is bigger? Which fear is more powerful?

1. The fear of change?

2. The fear of being left behind?

One of these fears will dominate. Which one will it be?

THE PAIN OF UNRESOLVED PROBLEMS

As humans, we think about our problems all day long. And for some of us? We worry about our problems well into the evening and then we can't sleep.

If our prospects worry about their problems all of the time, this should make our mind reading easy. What would be a good opening phrase that tells our prospects that not only do we read their minds, but that we also have empathy for their problems? Ready?

"It's tough."

Or, if we like bigger words, "It's difficult." Both phrases work. Let's do some examples.

- It's tough dealing with pain 24 hours a day.
- It's tough when our boss doesn't appreciate us at work.
- It's tough waking up to an alarm clock year after year.
- It's tough when we don't get paid what we are worth.
- It's tough when everything is so expensive.
- It's tough when we don't know what to do.
- It's tough when we don't have enough time.
- It's tough to diet when we are hungry.

Do we notice that not only are we reading their minds and having empathy, but we are also focusing and increasing their awareness of their problem?

Prospects want to solve their problems.

They don't want to keep them.

We can help.

BUT IT SEEMS IMPOSSIBLE TO READ MINDS

Ah, but we read minds all the time. Here is a simple example.

Our friend has an angry, twisted face. Is our friend thinking happy thoughts? Of course not. We automatically understand that our friend is thinking angry thoughts. Hopefully, the angry thoughts are not about us.

Without realizing it, we always try to figure out what other people are thinking and feeling. It's how we interact with others and build relationships. True, some of us are better at perception than others, but we all do some mind reading every time we interact with people. We look for a feeling of trust and mutual understanding that allows us to connect.

IS MIND READING A SKILL THAT CAN BE LEARNED?

Yes. Even if we feel we are currently clueless about what other people are thinking, we can get better at this. We can take our rapport-building to a higher level by improving our mind-reading skills. How? Here are some fast tips to make us better now.

1. PAY ATTENTION TO BODY LANGUAGE

Body language is a great way to get clues about what someone is thinking and feeling. Look for non-verbal signs of discomfort, such as crossed arms or legs, furrowed brows, wrinkled foreheads, clenched fists, tense muscles, or leaning away from us. These can be clues that our prospect is feeling uncomfortable or threatened by us. Maybe we never thought of ourselves as scary. Others might think we are scary, especially if we have salespeople's breath.

What is salespeople's breath? It is when salespeople are so hungry for a sales commission, they will say or do anything to get it. Prospects can smell salespeople's breath from a mile away.

But what is a good example of body language that can help us read minds?

Did we ever see someone smile? Does that give us a hint that they are having happy thoughts? It gets even better. We have the ability to distinguish the difference between a genuine smile and a forced smile. When someone gives us a forced, thin-lip smile, we know that is not a good sign.

Our prospects are fidgety. They tap their feet. Their faces look anxious. We read their minds. We know they think, "When will you shut up? We want to talk. We want to ask a question."

Do our prospects roll their eyes when we make our exaggerated claims? That is an obvious body language clue.

Do our prospects look at their phones when we talk? Uh-oh. Not a good sign. Our prospects think that we are boring and not worth their attention.

Prospects can only entertain one thought at a time in their minds. We want to make sure it is the thought we are sharing.

2. LISTEN FOR HOT BUTTONS

Ask engineers about the history of logarithmic slide rules. What happens? Their eyes light up. They become animated. They talk faster with traces of enthusiasm. It appears that the spirit of personality has entered their bodies. Would that give us a clue what they are thinking?

What if we are talking to old people, you know, those people over 30 years old? They smile when they talk about the old days when telephones had cords attached to the wall. They love to talk about the times when we didn't have pictures on social media of what their friends were eating. The times when we talked to each other instead of staring into our phone screens.

We see their thoughts turn inwards to that happy place in time. We make a mental note. If we talk more about traditional values instead of new technology and change, we will connect better.

What about prospects who talk to us in a boring monotone? Again, this is a hint.

If engineers can get excited about a topic, anyone can.

We need to be more interesting so that our monotone prospects come alive. This tells us that they have no passion for what we are talking about at this moment. Time for us to change to a different topic or benefit.

Want to go deeper?

Then, listen to not only what is being said, but "read between the lines." What is not being said could be more important. Now we are at the alpha level of listening skills.

3. BE A GREAT LISTENER

People love to talk. They will tell us exactly what is on their minds. How hard is that? All we have to do is shut up long enough and our prospects will tell us even their deepest, most secret thoughts. Listening helps us identify their hot buttons.

When we listen with acceptance, we gain their respect and trust. It is hard to listen without wanting to convince the other person about our opinions. Biting our tongue helps us keep quiet long enough so that we can understand what the other person is thinking.

Want to make this even better?

Try reflecting back or repeating what others tell us, just to make sure that we understand. This also gives us a chance to clarify our thoughts about what our prospects are thinking.

Normally people listen with the intention of what they are going to say next. They don't listen to the other person's message. Focusing on their message helps.

Want to make this better? Let's be aware that we currently use selective listening. We filter out what we don't want to hear, especially if it conflicts with the conversation inside of our heads. Yeah, we are normal. We have many cognitive biases.

4. USE OPEN-ENDED QUESTIONS

Asking questions is a fast way to get information from others. Police detectives love to ask open-ended questions. When suspects answer open-ended questions, they often incriminate themselves by revealing too much. Our prospects will do the same. As humans, we love to talk about ourselves. We are our favorite topic.

The more we understand our prospects, the better we can serve them.

Some of my favorite questions?

- How did you get into this type of career?
- What do you like best about your job?
- What do you like least about your job?
- What is the hardest part of dieting?
- When did you decide to start looking for a new car?
- Why did you choose Disney World instead of the beach?

The more our prospects talk, the more we understand.

5. OBSERVE OUR PROSPECTS' BASIC PERSONALITIES

If we are familiar with the four color personalities, we will know the default thinking patterns of our prospects and what motivates them. If we are not familiar with the four color personalities, here is a quick primer.

Yellow personalities find fulfillment in helping other people. Think massage therapists, kindergarten school teachers, and social workers. What is their default thinking pattern? Support, encouragement, teamwork, agreement, sharing, patience, trust, and cooperation. They want to know how what we offer can help others.

Blue personalities? Active versus passive. Talking versus listening. Excitement, new adventures, enthusiasm, and fun. Everyone knows at least one blue personality who is always talking, has a good story, and is a people person. We never have to read their minds. They are too busy telling us what's on their minds, usually with no filters.

Red personalities? These are bottom-line people who get things done. Results matter. They like to be the boss, to be in charge, and to tell other people what to do. Managers, politicians, and top sales leaders are red personalities. Their default thinking patterns? Strong-willed, lead the way, determined, competitive, and with little time for social chitchat. We know they are always thinking this, "Get to the point. Stop wasting time. Tell me the facts now. I don't have time to listen to waffling fluff. I have countries to conquer. Empires to build!"

Green personalities? These are our accountants, engineers, computer scientist, and generally boring people. They live for facts and data, and love to ask endless questions. Their main motive? To avoid making a bad decision. They have programs that tell them to delay any decision until every possible factor has been analyzed. What are they naturally thinking? "I need to be careful. I need to think of every possibility that could go wrong. I must avoid risk at all costs."

If we can determine our prospects' color personalities early in our conversation, we will know what thoughts to look for.

6. ANTICIPATE COMMON OBJECTIONS

We want to address our prospects' objections before they have a chance to raise them. Prevention is easier than a cure.

This is the reason for experience. If we gave 100 presentations and listed the common objections, we would know their possible objections before they raised them. We won't get this experience from sitting at home thinking about their objections. Real life is more accurate.

When done correctly, the conversation might sound like this.

Us: "You might be skeptical that this would work for you."

Prospect: "You're right. I am skeptical. I've heard too many horror stories of people who tried and failed. I was thinking just that."

Notice that we are still in rapport? No resistance. Prevention works.

7. ASK OUR PROSPECTS HOW THEY MADE A SIMILAR DECISION IN THE PAST

When we hear our prospects' stories, take notes. We want to learn from their past experiences of how they made decisions in the past.

- What are our prospects' patterns?
- What seemed most important?
- How long did it take?
- What was the reason that triggered their final decision?

Again, our prospect is telling us exactly what is going on inside of their minds.

8. LET'S TAKE A LESSON FROM HYPNOSIS

Think about a hypnosis session. During hypnosis, our minds are open and we accept new suggestions with ease. Why is this?

Because the trained hypnotist knows to start with our current beliefs. Current beliefs? Well, our hypnotist will be using statements that are likely to be true of almost anyone.

Our hypnotist might say something like this, "As you are sitting here today, in this comfortable chair, listening to the chirping birds outside this window ..."

What is our natural reaction? We think, "Yes, I am sitting here today. Yes, this chair is very comfortable. Yes, those birds are chirping."

We feel that the hypnotist understands us. We feel that the hypnotist sees and understands the world from our viewpoint. We can accept what the hypnotist tells us next, as long as it is not too far from reality.

Hypnotism is the ultimate rapport. We give up our skepticism, relax, and accept new suggestions and facts.

What did the hypnotist do? The hypnotist read our minds. "Reading our minds" was nothing more than observing the obvious.

If the hypnotist wishes to take us deeper into hypnosis, there would be more statements that we would agree with. Maybe the hypnotist would continue with obvious facts such as, "This is a warm summer day."

And now, some magic.

Our hypnotist could calmly ask, "Tell me about your favorite vacation spot."

With our eyes closed, we transfer ourselves back to that place in time and relive those happy moments. All our hypnotist has to do is take notes, and now he understands more about that happy place in our minds.

Hypnotists are great listeners. If we wish to have superhuman mind-reading powers, we will want to develop superhuman listening powers. We do not need to put people into trances, but we do need to listen for the clues that tell us what is going on in their minds.

And then, repeat.

After we read our prospects' minds, we can repeat what we heard. This tells our prospects we understand them. Some examples of what we could say?

- I see that you are a practical person.
- It sounds like you really want to lose weight.
- I see that you love your family.
- It sounds like you feel stressed about this problem.
- You impress me as someone who wants to get ahead.
- You certainly are a person who takes good care of your health.
- I see that you are very careful about risk.

How can our prospects argue with what they told us?

Want to make it unbelievably easier? Say this.

"Based on what you told me, I feel you are thinking …"

We will sound so professional!

WHAT ARE WE THINKING?

If we are like most marketing professionals, we are thinking, "What are some great common facts that I can start with that will help my prospects relax and listen with an open mind?"

To come up with these common facts, all we have to do is start thinking like our prospects. Let's learn and practice that skill now.

MIND READING IN ACTION

Chicago, 1975.

It is early on a Sunday evening. My phone rings and the caller is upset. "You need to come downtown to the Holiday Inn immediately. We have a problem. And it is your problem."

Well, that didn't sound good. I was just a small-time network marketer trying to build my business with home meetings. I wasn't sure why a big-time company like the Holiday Inn would be calling me. But, this wasn't feeling good.

I drove downtown and walked into the lobby.

Uh-oh.

Standing room only. Angry people shouting. A riot ready to explode.

I work my way through the crowd at the front desk and introduced myself. The manager quickly took me to the back room.

"What is going on out there?" I asked.

"It's your people," the manager said.

"My people? I don't have any people here."

"Your staff told me it is all your fault?"

"Staff? I don't have any …"

And then I saw someone I recognized. Ah, the "staff" was one of my new downline distributors. He was shaking and apologized. "I didn't know it would turn out like this! Honestly!"

The crowd got louder. It wasn't looking good.

So I asked my new distributor, "What did you do?"

He stuttered, "My friend knows a popular disc jockey, so I got some free advertising on his radio show earlier today. I had the disc jockey announce, 'Jobs! Jobs! Jobs for everyone! Come to the Holiday Inn this evening at 6 pm to get your job!'"

With that explanation, my distributor announced, "I quit. This business isn't for me. I am out of here!"

The Holiday Inn staff released him and glared at me. "What are you going to do about this?" The crowd's shouting got louder. My now-retired distributor had reserved a small meeting room for interviewing the applicants. But with 200+ mad people in the lobby, there was no way that was going to work. I had to think quickly.

"Give me the ballroom quick. Get them out of your lobby. I can't talk to them there." I hoped this gave me time to think. The manager said, "Sure. Get them out of the lobby. And there will be a charge for the ballroom too!"

"No problem," I said. I would worry about that later. The mob moved to the ballroom.

Gang members, unemployed teenagers, and mothers on welfare rushed into the ballroom.

As I walked to the front of the ballroom, I wondered what I could do next. People were upset, shouting, and ready to fight. It looked like a losing battle. But then I had an idea.

TRY SOME MIND READING SKILLS!

If I could read their minds, they might be quiet long enough to hear a few words of my message. This would get me permission for a few more words before they would interrupt. I needed time to calm them down. I needed time to explain.

If I couldn't read their minds, they would attack.

Some self-appointed mob leader yelled, "Quiet! Quiet! He is going to talk,"

Mind reading ... this had better be good. One chance. No do-overs. I started.

"How many of you are here for the job?" Hands went up. A few people whispered, "Shhhhh." They wanted to hear what I would say next.

"I know many of you spent your last few dollars on bus fare to get here tonight." Several people in the audience grumbled in agreement.

"And, I understand that many of you are angry. You feel like you've been lied to." A few people shouted in agreement, with some extra four-letter words thrown in.

"Most people want to know what is going on and what we can do to help you get jobs." A few boos and some more shouting, but at least I was getting a few words in.

"So you are probably wondering what I can do to help." Yeah, they were wondering.

The mind reading was working.

The crowd put their "pitchforks and torches" away for the moment, to hear what I would say to fix this ugly situation.

"I can't give you a job. But, I might be able to help you get a job." I was struggling, but the crowd was listening. They wanted to hear more. I had their attention.

THE RESULT?

A happy ending? No.

It was still humiliating, embarrassing, and ugly, but not life-threatening. I committed to helping them get jobs, reimbursed some bus fare, apologized profusely, and left the hotel that evening with high blood pressure. Then I watched television non-stop for a few days to recover.

But I learned many lessons.

First? Hostile crowds. Definitely not my favorite thing. Most hostile crowds won't even let us start. They want to heckle and shout their opinions and hate. To combat this, we have to act fast.

If our hostile crowd senses any weakness, lack of confidence, or that we don't think as they do, it is over. Even our best logical facts won't be heard. Unless there is rapport, our message dies. Our message will never enter their brains.

Second? How many words do we have to win over a hostile crowd or a skeptical prospect? Five words? Ten words? We are going to be judged, and judged harshly. No time for idle chit-chat and small talk.

Third? Use words and phrases that match the emotions that are in their minds now. More about that in a bit.

With hostile crowds or prospects, starting with a mind reading statement is the best way for our message to be heard.

TEN WORDS

"As you are sitting here today, you are probably wondering ..."

Think about what happens when we say these ten words to a group of prospects at our opportunity presentation.

What are our prospects thinking? "Yes, we are sitting here today. And yes, we were wondering ..."

Of course, our prospects are wondering. That is what humans do when we don't know what is going to happen next.

Is this the best way to start with a hostile crowd? Not sure. There could be better ways, but this way at least has a chance of working.

We are not trained hypnotists, but we do know the importance of mind reading and rapport. How would we continue our opportunity presentation? It would sound like this.

"As you are sitting here today, you are probably wondering ..." and then, let's fill in the rest of our opening sentence. Here are some options.

- How long will this last?
- How much longer can we put up with this problem?
- When is our next break?
- Will I have to pay for lunch?
- Are you for or against this proposal?
- How expensive is this going to be?
- How is this even possible? Are you sure?
- What will others think if I do this?
- Can I do this? What are my chances of success?

- Is there some sort of guarantee? I don't want to take any risk.

Oh, my. Lots of possibilities. The easiest way to mind reading a hostile audience is to think of their skepticism. When people fold their arms, or wrinkle their foreheads, we know they are skeptical. It should not be hard to guess their objections.

Mind reading our prospects' objections can change their viewpoint about us. We can get upgraded from a pushy salesperson to a trusted advisor.

BUT HOW WILL WE KNOW WHAT OUR PROSPECTS ARE THINKING?

Imagine our perfect prospect.

- What is our perfect prospect like?
- What does our perfect prospect do every day?
- What does our perfect prospect want in his or her life?
- What is our prospect's biggest problem or challenge?
- What goes through our prospect's mind right now?

We want to imagine one person who would represent our market. If we can visualize this person in our minds, this will be the beginning step of our mind reading.

Now, let's put ourselves in our prospect's shoes. Maybe it will help if we describe our ideal prospect a bit more. Let's ask ourselves some more specific questions.

- What does our prospect do for work?
- What is our prospect's job title?
- What is the prospect's biggest challenge at work?

- What does the prospect want to achieve in his or her career?

- Does our prospect have to endure long commutes to work?

- Is our prospect worried about reputation or status?

- Is there a conflict with the boss?

Once we have a true vision of our prospect, it will be easier to have empathy and see the world through our prospect's eyes. The next obvious question is, "What is my prospect thinking right now?"

This is simple to do. Allow our imagination to jump into our prospect's mind for 24 hours and think about how this person sees the world.

Start with the morning routine. What happens when our prospect wakes up in the morning? What is the first thing that he or she thinks about? Does our prospect have a family? If so, how does our prospect interact with his or her spouse and children? What are some of the problems that our prospect deals with on a daily basis?

This is a fun exercise that forces even the coldest salesperson into empathy.

Now, let's move on.

LET'S GO DEEPER

We know our prospects and how our prospects feel. Let's go deeper now into the problems our prospects have.

The challenge with problems is that they are too general. This is our time to focus and get specific. Imagine this example of a problem.

"I don't have enough money."

Is that what our prospects think about this problem? No, this is too general. Instead, our prospects think in specifics, such as:

- I don't have enough money to send my daughter to a private school.
- Why is it I can barely afford the minimum credit card payments?
- Buying food is too expensive now.
- I can't believe the cost to fill my car with fuel.
- How can I invest in my future if I can't even pay today's bills?

Of course, these thoughts don't all have to be negative. Let's put a positive spin on how our prospects might visualize their problems.

- What kind of vacation could I take if I had the money?
- It would be fun to afford to golf every Saturday.
- I want an awesome car so that I look better to my neighbors.
- What would life be like if I could sleep until 9 am?
- I wonder if I could get back to my High School weight.
- Imagine how I would make those former cheerleaders jealous by showing up to the class reunion with no wrinkles.

WHY ARE WE SPENDING SO MUCH EMPHASIS ON SPECIFICS?

Because specifics generate emotions. And as we know, emotions generate decisions and actions.

Problems naturally create emotions. Our prospects' subconscious minds think in emotions and feelings, not words.

So our next step?

Imagine the "feelings and emotions" our prospects have when they think of their problems.

Let's imagine some feelings for our frustrated, hard-working, long-commuting, prospect. Ready?

- Happy
- Sad
- Frustrated
- Angry
- Anxious
- Insecure
- Tired
- Lonely
- Jealous
- Revenge

Enough emotions? I am sure we could think of more.

Ask ourselves:

- How do my prospects feel when they experience their problems?
- What would be different if they didn't have these problems?
- How do they feel about other things they have tried that didn't work?
- What do my prospects feel would be the ideal outcome?
- Now that we think we know their feelings and emotions, it is time to find out for sure. How?

HOW TO FIND OUT THE EXACT EMOTIONS?

Let's talk to a few of our prospects. Take the time to engage in conversation and listen closely to what they say, and how they phrase it. The exact words they use will be valuable for us. We know these words will connect quickly inside our prospects' minds when we repeat them later.

How else can we find out specific problems and the exact words prospects use to describe their emotions? How about a little research?

Are there online groups and forums with people who have these problems? Spend a little time reading what they complain about, and see if they expose their feelings also. Maybe there are community groups where we can listen for more problems.

How else could we get this inside information?

Talk to professionals who deal with our typical prospects every day. What do our prospects say or confide to them? What are the most common complaints? The most common requests?

Or, researching this information could be as easy as observing the complaints in our social media newsfeeds. People love to complain.

We will talk more about how to research later. But for now, ask ourselves this question.

HOW WRONG CAN WE BE?

Really wrong!

When I started network marketing, I talked to hundreds of prospects. No one joined. That is what we call a hint.

The problem was that I saw the world from my point of view. As a shy, nerdy, personality-free, engineer personality, I gave prospects fact after fact after fact. I loved the data and proof. I thought not having enough facts held my prospects back from making a decision.

Was I wrong? Very wrong.

How did I know? Because when no one joined, I decided to give my prospects even more facts, and still no one joined. Sometimes proof stares us in the face.

What were these non-engineer prospects thinking? Were they thinking they needed additional facts? No.

They were thinking this:

- What will my friends think about me?
- Do I have to be a salesperson?
- What if I get rejected?
- What if my friends think I am stupid?
- Am I making a mistake here?
- I don't know enough people?
- How am I going to find enough people to talk to?
- Why should I take a chance, this might be risky?

Because I saw the world from my viewpoint, I had no empathy for my prospects. I missed out on a chance to do basic minor reading and create better rapport. It is obvious to me now why no one signed up. True incompetence prevents prospects from moving forward with us.

CONNECTION

When we understand our prospects' thoughts, problems, and emotions, we will have empathy. This will create a solid connection and establish rapport with our prospects.

Will our prospects notice that we care? Absolutely! They will feel and appreciate our empathy.

Is this hard? No. We can follow the steps in this chapter and master this mind reading skill.

As a final caution, remember there is a huge difference between empathy and sympathy.

Empathy means we understand the feelings of others.

This doesn't mean we have these feelings ourselves. We don't have to have the same feelings as our prospects to understand them. We don't have to agree with their feelings to understand them. Empathy means we are aware of their feelings.

Sympathy means we have the same feelings as others.

This may mean that we feel pity or sorrow for someone. If we are sympathetic we might be tempted to give unsolicited advice. Probably not a good idea.

Let's strive for empathy.

We want to read and understand the thoughts of our prospects.

THE CONNECTION

How will prospects know that we can read their minds and have empathy for them?

By demonstration. We make a simple statement about them that is true. They think, "You understand me. You are not talking AT me. You are talking WITH me. You are in my world."

Now for the good news!

The safe statements we use could be true for most people. We don't have to be mind reading experts. We only have to demonstrate we understand them.

Examples of safe statements?

- "I feel your family is very important to you."
- "You seem to be careful about how you spend your money."
- "I see you have a passion for good health."
- "I can see that you are a very busy person."
- "I understand that you want the best for your children."
- "You probably care a lot about others' feelings."
- "I know you are a practical person."

Notice how these statements are about our prospects, not about us or what we offer. This is a difference between amateurs and professionals.

Amateurs talk to prospects about their companies' features, benefits, awards, and other boring topics. Prospects don't care about these things. They don't care about us, and they care even less about what we represent.

What do your prospects care about? Themselves. Yes, they are selfish, self-centered, and totally focused on their world. This is why amateurs struggle so much. Amateurs show their videos, PowerPoint presentations, brochures, and testimonials. But as Steven Burke says, "Videos and PowerPoint presentations don't listen."

Prospects want us to talk about them instead of what we represent. Prospects want us to discuss their struggles, problems, and lives.

Empathy is a superpower that we get from practicing our mind reading skills. This programs our minds to see the important picture: "It is all about helping our prospects."

We want to leave behind our marketing jargon, brochures, PowerPoint presentations, and company videos. They clutter our minds and keep us from connecting with our prospects. If our conversations are with prospects, we will be successful. We don't want to be reading advertising and promotional facts to our prospects.

The big lesson?

When we can read minds, we can change minds.

THE TWO-WORD SHORTCUT

Sound too good to be true? Two words?

We can read our prospects' minds with almost 100% certainty. Their internal thoughts start with the words, "I want."

Think of conversations similar to a negotiation. Each party wants something. And what do our human minds want? Here are some obvious wants:

- Security
- Food
- Money
- Power
- Good health
- More desserts
- To be loved
- To sleep later in the morning
- No more commuting
- Respect from others
- Recognition, and more

Our human minds think about our wants every waking moment. So as soon as we are in conversation with prospects, this happens.

First, they think, "What do I want from this conversation." Yes, they are not worried about us. They have their own self-interests.

Second, they think, "How can I get you to give me what I want?"

Again, our prospects are not concerned about us. They want to know how they can get what they want.

Imagine this scenario.

Us: "I could show you the entire company presentation, but I know that isn't what you want to hear. You are interested in how you can work from home, instead of fighting traffic, right?"

Prospect: "You're right. I am skeptical when I see presentations. I've seen too many sales pitches before."

Hmmm. This is going in a good direction. Our mind reading is working.

HOW TO SOUND LIKE A PROFESSIONAL

It is not hard to imagine what our prospects want. The words inside of their heads start with, "I want."

So, what can we say that will demonstrate our high-level mind reading powers?

Three words. "How you can …"

Isn't that what they would love to hear next? Of course. Let's do a couple of examples.

Example #1. Work from home.

We know our prospect is thinking, "I want to work from my home. I hate waking up early and commuting in bumper-to-bumper traffic." This wasn't hard to determine, we just listened. Now, what will we say next?

Here is the before and after of what we can say.

Before: "Let me tell you about our wonderful business. You can even work this business from your home." (Not bad, but we can do better.)

After: "You are probably wondering **how you can** wake up late and work from home." (Better.)

Our prospect thinks, "Yes. That is exactly what I was thinking. Please continue."

By adjusting a couple of words, we connect with the conversation in our prospect's head. Now our prospect is looking forward to more from us.

Example #2. My schedule stinks.

We know our prospect is thinking, "I hate my alarm. I am not a morning person. Monday through Friday is torture."

This wasn't hard to determine, because we listened. Now, what will we say next?

Here is the before.

Before: "Let me tell you about our wonderful business. You can build it to a full-time income and then wake up when you want." (Not bad, but we can do better.)

After: "You are probably wondering **how you can** work from home, set your own hours, and wake up when you are tired of sleeping." (Better.)

Our prospect thinks, "Yes. That is exactly what I was thinking. Please continue."

Connection. Our prospect is asking us to continue. We aren't pitching a business. We answer our prospect's most pressing question. We have our prospect's attention.

Example #3. Fire my dream-sucking, selfish boss.

We know our prospect is thinking, "I want to fire my boss. He is a dream-sucking, selfish jerk that doesn't care about me. I work hard and do everything he asks, but it is never enough."

This wasn't hard to guess, we just listened to our prospect's rants and complaints. Now, what will we say next?

Here is the before and after of what we can say.

Before: "Let me tell you about our wonderful business. This is your chance to be your own boss." (Not bad, but we can do better.)

After: "I know you want to know **how you can** fire your boss and be the boss." (Better.)

Again, our prospect feels a deeper connection with us.

Example #4. I need more money as my family's expenses are more than my paycheck.

We know our prospect is thinking, "I want more money. My credit card balances keep growing. I can't get ahead financially with my paycheck."

Listening made this easy. This is why listeners do better than talkers in sales. It is hard to know the deepest desires of our prospects if we are doing all the talking.

Here is the before and after of what we can say.

Before: "Let me tell you about our wonderful business. You can make extra money with our company." (Not bad, but we can do better.)

After: "You are probably thinking about **how you can** get an extra paycheck every week, so you can pay off debt fast and get ahead." (Better.)

Our prospect thinks, "Well, I was thinking something close to that. This sounds interesting. Tell me more."

Example #5. I don't want to be a salesperson.
We know our prospect is thinking, "I want to avoid rejection. I don't want my family to think I am a sleazy, pushy salesperson. Begging my friends to buy from me will drive them away."

Many people have this internal program. If our prospect is shy, we know our prospect is thinking this.

Here is the before and after of what we can say.

Before: "Let me tell you about our wonderful business. You don't have to be a salesperson. We believe in sharing and caring." (Not bad, but we can do better.)

After: "You might be wondering **how you can** avoid rejection and still build a successful business." (Better.)

Our prospect thinks, "That is exactly what I want to know!"

With the proper words, mind reading is so easy.

"HOW YOU CAN ..."

By placing these words in our opening sentence, we can create an instant connection. And did we notice that we talked about our prospects, and not about ourselves?

Mind reading is not reciting a PowerPoint presentation or sending prospects to a video. Mind reading is talking about the conversation that is already inside of our prospect's minds.

LET'S PRACTICE OUR MIND READING POWERS NOW

Imagine we are in front of a group of people who lost their jobs today. The organizer asks us to speak to this newly unemployed group. But what do we see?

Folded arms. Empty faces of despair. Bored, broken spirits. And, no one is smiling. Doesn't look good. Tough audience.

Time to put our mind reading superpowers to work. What is our negative audience thinking? (This should be easy for us by now.)

- "I need a job."
- "I'm never going to find a job."
- "I feel numb."
- "Nobody is going to want to hire me."
- "I have to find a job fast."
- "I need to start looking for a job now, so why am I sitting here listening to a stranger?"

We could start our talk with the obvious, "I know the #1 thing on our minds right now is how you can get another job."

What would be the reactions in their minds? They would think, "Yeah. That's right. Tell me more."

And at that moment, we opened their minds to hear our second sentence.

Doesn't this sound like a better way to start instead of talking about our wonderful qualifications? Oh yeah. We remembered. They don't care about us.

Should we mind read a little deeper? What else could they be thinking?

- "I can't believe this happened to me."
- "Why did this happen to me?"
- "What am I going to do?"
- "I didn't expect this."
- "I don't know what to think."
- "This is so unfair."

What could we say next to show that we read these thoughts in their minds? Possibly we could continue with, "And I know we wonder what we will do next?"

That wasn't hard to do. More connection with our audience.

We only need a couple of sentences to signal to our audience that we understand them, and have empathy with their situation. We don't need to be trained hypnotists. We don't need a psychology degree. If we care about people, this feels natural.

Let's read their minds a little deeper. Ready?

- "I don't know where to begin."
- "I'm not qualified for anything."
- "I'm too old to start over."
- "I have to support my family."
- "I don't even know how to apply for another job."

Do we now feel empathy? Do we feel their problems and concerns? Now we know how to connect.

But, let's go deeper into their minds. Many in the audience will be feeling these thoughts:

- "I'm never going to make it."
- "Everything is going to be so hard now."
- "I'm in so much trouble."
- "This is a nightmare."
- "How will I pay my mortgage?"
- "I'm going to lose everything."
- "I'm not good enough."

We know what we should be talking about. We know what our message should be. A canned presentation would be ignored. But now, with us talking directly to their minds, we can get our message inside of their heads. They will want to listen.

Deeper? Should we go really deep? Go into their darkest emotions about this problem? Let's do it. Here are their deeper thoughts:

- "I'm a failure."
- "I'm so confused."
- "I'm so stressed out."
- "I feel so overwhelmed."
- "I'm so lost."
- "I feel so hopeless."
- "I need help."
- "I'm so scared."
- "I'm going to end up alone."

- "I'm going to be homeless."

Yikes! This feels depressing. But isn't that what we would feel if we lost our jobs?

Sure, some people will say that losing their job is a great opportunity to move forward. But that is not the usual first response. Our human survival program quickly panics if we lose our current job unexpectedly.

WHAT IS THE BIG LESSON FROM THIS CASE STUDY?

First, by understanding our prospects' thoughts, we can better understand their emotions. If we know their emotions, then we can more easily appeal to them.

Second, by understanding their thoughts, we know what content to give them. We don't want to waste their time talking about irrelevant information that doesn't apply to what is on their minds.

Third, by understanding their thoughts, we can better understand how to connect with them. This is the purpose of mind reading. We want to have a clear connection so our ultimate message will be heard.

READY TO DO ONE MORE CASE STUDY?

Imagine we are at an appointment with a husband and wife who expressed interest in our business opportunity. Things are a little cold. Everything feels formal and not relaxed.

We think to ourselves, "What is going on inside their minds?"

Stop here for a moment. Can we imagine what they are thinking? Can we feel empathy for their distrust and fear? Let's make a mental list of their thoughts before we read further.

\<Pause.\>

\<Pause.\>

\<Pause.\>

\<Keep thinking.\>

\<Pause.\>

Okay. How was our mind reading session? Let's compare our mental checklist with some of the following thoughts. Ready?

- "I don't know if we can trust you."
- "You don't know our situation."
- "Are you a salesperson?"
- "We better look for something bad in your presentation, so we have ammunition to fight off your power close at the end when you corner us for a money investment."

Yikes! That went downhill fast. Some powerful emotions from our prospects. Their last thought? "We better look for something bad in your presentation, so we have ammunition to fight off your power close at the end when you corner us for a money investment."

We sense this negative thought by their skeptical faces and the daggers coming from their eyes. Extremely defensive already. They must have had a bad experience with a salesperson recently.

We think, "I better take care of that objection immediately. If I don't break through that fear, they won't believe another word I say." So here is how we start.

"First, I want you to know that it is perfectly okay to ignore this part-time business opportunity and keep your situation the same. Many people do. It is also okay to take advantage of this part-time business. Many people do that also. But please remember that you are in charge of your choices. You know your situation better than anyone else. So, would you like to know the details about this part-time business?"

So much happens here. They learn not to be afraid. No one is going to high-pressure close them at the end. They feel good that the choice is all theirs. No judgment from us. We even confirmed this by letting them know they have the inside information about their personal situation that no one else has. Only they are qualified to make a decision.

Did we also notice that we presented our opportunity as an option, not as a presentation to be sold? People love options. Think of the difference between these two words: presentation and options.

"Presentation" means a salesperson is going to try to close them at the end. Look for negatives.

"Options" mean that the only way this can benefit them is if they can find a way to make it work for them. Now they are looking for reasons why this will work, instead of why it will not work.

With this first barrier out of the way, they will listen to the next words we say. Remember, this is all we ask. We want them to hear our message without prejudice and filters, so they can make the best decision for their lives.

Do we feel scared that they might choose not to do our business? Think of it this way. The wonderful offer of our wonderful business certainly looks like a better option for them than keeping their lives the same. Most people will want what we have to offer. And those that don't? Well, we are sure they have a legitimate reason to hold back. That is okay, we respect that.

But let's continue. What other thoughts do they have that we can mind read?

- "Will we be comfortable with this business?"
- "Do we have to be salespeople?"
- "Will you ask us to contact and harass our friends?"
- "Is this an illegal pyramid?"
- "What if it isn't for us? Will you leave us alone?"
- "What will our in-laws think?"
- "Will anyone buy what we offer? Is there a market?"
- "Will this be too expensive?"
- "We don't have time for this. We are too busy even now."
- "Do we have to quit our jobs?"
- "Will there be a catch at the end?"

Looks like we have a few more objections to address before we get to our presentation. Our prospects will appreciate that we talk about what worries them first.

We won't have to address all these thoughts, but if we address a few of them, we will signal to our prospects our empathy.

This shouldn't be hard to predict their thoughts. Why? Because we had the same feelings when we joined. Mind reading is easy.

This gets even better. We are talking to our prospects in conversation, not reading a script. This feels natural so we will have less resistance from our prospects.

WHERE ELSE CAN WE PRACTICE OUR MIND READING SKILLS?

With our coworkers. With our children or grandchildren. With our neighbors. With our boss? Even our pets. This gets to be so much fun.

We could sit at a sidewalk café with a nice cup of coffee, imagining the thoughts of the people passing by. Practicing can be a lot of fun.

What might be the biggest takeaways from this mind reading lesson?

To listen more.

To listen before we speak.

To listen to gather clues about what is on our prospects' minds.

WE MIND READ PROSPECTS NOW

Have we ever been in a conversation and felt we knew what the other person was going to say next? Then, we were mind reading.

Have we ever interrupted people and finished their sentences for them? Yes, it is rude, but we knew what they were going to say, and decided we would finish the sentence for them. Again, we were mind reading.

Wait! We have been doing these things all our lives. We just didn't call it mind reading.

Mind reading isn't mystical. It's a daily skill everyone uses. The good news is that the more we consciously practice mind reading, the better we get.

JANE VS. GRUMPY

Jane starts her sales presentation, but immediately feels something is wrong. Her prospect is leaning backward, not forward. Not a good sign. And the wrinkles forming on her prospect's forehead appear ominous. Oh no! Now her prospect starts to roll his eyes. This is going downhill fast.

Jane tries to focus, but it is hard with her prospect signaling he isn't interested in what she has to say. She needs a breakthrough. She needs to impress her prospect by reading his mind. Unless she can get some respect, her words will fade into the ether, never to be heard by her prospect.

She takes a deep breath, trying to focus on what her intuition is whispering to her about this grumpy prospect. Suddenly, inspiration strikes! It's time to put her mind reading skills on steroids.

She stares directly into her prospect's eyes, pauses, and leans forward.

With confidence, she announces, "I can tell that you're not impressed, but I can change that."

Her prospect's eyes widen, and his body snaps to attention. "What makes you say that? How can you be so sure you can read my mind?"

Jane smiles. "Well, your body language is hurting my eyes, and the skeptical wrinkles on your forehead are so deep, they are creating shadows. And I understand why you would be skeptical."

"You understand?" Jane's prospect was listening.

"I understand I'm taking up valuable time you need for your business today. Most people in your situation wish I would stop and go away, so they can get back to more pressing work. But I only want to interrupt your day for two minutes. I want to show you how my product can help you live longer, so you will live extra days to do even more business. I am thinking that living extra days in your life is important, right?"

"Uh, yes. So continue." Jane's prospect was intrigued.

With her prospect's permission and attention, Jane continues her presentation.

The victory goes to Jane on this one. Mind reading to the rescue.

RESEARCH

As salespeople, one of our most important jobs is to figure out what our prospects' problems and desires are. Only then can we offer them a solution that fits their needs. But how do we go about researching this information? Here are ten resource ideas on where to research our prospects so that we can find out their deepest desires.

RESEARCH IDEA #1: USE SURVEYS

Do we have to stand on a street corner with a clipboard and stop strangers? We could, but for many of us, this would be outside of our comfort zone. And, random strangers may not be in touch with the feelings and problems of our target market. Collecting opinions from people who can't relate won't help us. Then, where can we get people to fill out our surveys? The Internet and social media can give us instant feedback. Our target market may be thrilled to have their opinions known. Several social media platforms have polls built-in, so it is easy to get feedback with a few clicks of the mouse.

Here is an example of surveys helping us understand what our prospects are thinking.

Imagine a local online poll that asks, "Why would you want a part-time business?" We could offer four options.

A. Need the extra money

B. I am bored and want something to do

C. A chance to grow a part-time business so that I can eventually be my own boss

D. Tax advantages

If we are smart, we would allow the readers to create and add their own options. Maybe our four choices are not the only choices. What happens?

Many voters write in this option, "To have a second paycheck in case the factory closes."

Oh? We didn't know about this motivation. We didn't know the factory's future was in doubt. By adding this to our conversations with local prospects, they feel we have mind reading powers. They feel we understand their situation.

RESEARCH IDEA #2: NETWORKING GROUPS.

People with common interest band together for meetings and discussions. Whether in-person or virtual, these networking groups can give us a wealth of information about their needs. Social media platforms and organizations come and go. Here are a few ideas of where to start.

LinkedIn has many industry-specific groups. Think of all of the Facebook groups. In-person groups? Meetup.com and the BNI breakfast get-togethers will find like-minded people for many of us. Attending these meetings in person can introduce us to people who can help with our research.

An example of how connecting with this group can give us better insights into their wants and needs?

A local poker group meets every Thursday evening. Mostly men. The local skincare and make-up salesperson thinks, "Hey. I will give them my catalog. They can take the catalog home, show it to their wives, and maybe I'll get some orders." Bad assumption.

What does she discover? The men don't want to give a catalog to their wives. Instead, they want her to pick out a gift package of her products that they can give their wives. They don't know how to shop, are afraid of shopping, and every gift they bought their wife previously was returned. They figure buying from the local skincare and make-up salesperson will give them a better chance of an appropriate gift.

The make-up and skincare salesperson's new one-line mind reading script?

"Let me be your personal shopper for all of your gift-giving needs."

RESEARCH IDEA #3: PUT THE INTERNET TO USE AS OUR RESEARCH ASSISTANT.

Google Search can kickstart some research. By looking for keywords related to our market, we can read what concerns are on their minds. If we want to be notified whenever someone talks about our topic, we can sign up for Google Alerts. We'll get a notification whenever our topic is mentioned online.

Or simply go to a Q & A site such as Quora. Tens of thousands of people volunteer their questions and their expert opinion answers. There is something for every topic.

An example of how Internet research can give us better insights into our prospects' wants and needs?

A vitamin salesperson tells prospects to purchase vitamins to live longer and to build their immune system. But are those the only reasons people should take vitamins? Of course not. But what are the other reasons? A short search on the Internet and look at all the additional reasons prospects want to add vitamins to their diets.

1. They worry about their bones getting old
2. Help regulate their blood pressure
3. To feel better about themselves when eating fast-food
4. Poor eating habits
5. They heard flu season is coming
6. They think they will sleep better at night
7. Seems easier than exercise

Mind reading? Connecting?

Now our vitamin salesperson says, "Exercise is hard and takes time. But in case you can't exercise, at least take these vitamins, so you will be doing something good for your health."

Think of the people who don't exercise. A huge market.

RESEARCH IDEA #4: MARKETPLACES SUCH AS AMAZON.COM HAVE REVIEWS FROM THEIR CUSTOMERS.

We will want to read the one, two, and three-star reviews to see what made these customers unhappy. Complainers take time out of their day to list their biggest irritations. Since the purpose of business is to solve other people's problems, this information is gold to us.

Here is a research example.

A stainless-steel cookware salesperson reads the negative reviews from ceramic cookware buyers. He discovers that many people are unhappy with the way their ceramic cookware scratches, chips, doesn't conduct heat evenly, and can't handle high temperatures. The cookware salesperson's presentation is almost writing itself.

"I know you worry about investing a lot of money in cookware. You worry about scratches, chips, and are afraid that high heat will ruin the cookware. That is why we don't sell ceramic cookware, but only stainless-steel cookware. You can cook and enjoy, not cook and worry."

How will the prospect feel? Great. So much covered in only four sentences.

RESEARCH IDEA #5: LOOK TO OUR INDUSTRY'S THOUGHT LEADERS.

They know our target market and their most pressing questions and needs. These thought leaders have books, lectures, videos, podcast interviews, and blog posts. Think of the thousands of hours they have with our target market. Their professional insights can tell us exactly what is on our prospects' minds. After only a few minutes of reading or listening, we should be hooked. Their insights should be fascinating to us.

A research example? We want to know why people hate their jobs but don't do anything to change. Here is what we find.

People get comfortable. They are afraid of change. Maybe their new boss will be worse. Because they are unsure of the future, they do nothing. Worse yet, what if they quit their jobs and can't find another job? Security is important to them.

Now that we know their fears, our offer is clear. We tell our prospects how starting a part-time business won't interfere with their current job. Now their objections melt away. We mind read their biggest fears, and tell them how our opportunity won't threaten their security.

Less stress. Better understanding. Rapport. And a great connection with our prospects.

RESEARCH IDEA #6: OUR COMPETITION HAS A HEAD START ON FIGURING OUT WHAT OUR TARGET MARKET WANTS.

We can learn from their mistakes and successes. Their professional marketing materials can tell us what they think is inside our target market's minds. Check out their web page, their sales pages, their brochures, their posts, and any other content they produce.

The example? Suppose that we sell diet products.

We go to our competitor's website and find this headline: "Lose 12 pounds by Friday!"

We know that is a ridiculous promise. But what does their headline tell us? They know what is going on inside their target market's minds. They know their chubby prospects want a quick fix so that they can go back to eating deep-fried pizza. The market wants instant results with little or no effort.

We adjust our message. "No promises. No hype. Real results you can see instantly with our diet products. We even include a free tape measure so you can measure your real results every Saturday. Let your chubby friends believe the silly hype. But you? You will have the results that will make them jealous."

Now we sound like the rational voice of authority. We will inspire more confidence by talking to the thoughts in their minds.

RESEARCH IDEA #7: TRADE SHOWS ATTRACT GREAT PROSPECTS, BRINGING THEM TO OUR TABLE OR BOOTH.

The next step is up to us. How well will we engage them? What will we learn from this brief social engagement?

The best part of trade shows? Other vendors. As they travel from city to city, they get vast amounts of experience and input from their tradeshow visitors. We can find them eating junk food at the concessions, and even at the bar later that evening. Why not invite one of them for dinner and have a deeper discussion of what is in our prospects' minds?

Need an example?

At a trade show in Chicago, I took a fellow vendor to dinner that evening. He had 15+ years of experience at these city-to-city business opportunity trade shows.

He told me, "People come here hoping to buy a business that requires no promotion or selling. They are scared to sell. They want to avoid the hard work of building a business. They are looking for a magic business where customers come to them, pre-sold. So, I tell them to buy my business opportunity because it sells itself. They just need to sit back and take the money."

I am thinking, "Ouch. That seems deceptive. But he does have a point. People at these shows don't want to be salespeople. They have a fear of selling conversation going on inside of their heads."

With that insight into my prospects' thoughts, I adjusted how I explained selling in my business. I then told my prospects, "You don't have to be a salesperson, but you do have to let people know about this product. Let them decide if they need it or not. Just don't keep the product secret. They will instantly know if they need it now ... or not."

This made my prospects feel better. They could visualize introducing my product, and then allow their prospects to volunteer if they were interested.

RESEARCH IDEA #8: YOUTUBE.COM HAS MILLIONS OF VIDEOS FROM PEOPLE WHO WANT TO BE ON CAMERA.

They are eager to share their stories and their lives with others. We can get an encyclopedia of information by listening to their opinions and findings. If we are perceptive, we can pick up their emotions behind the raw facts. Their emotions could lead us to what triggers their buying decisions.

Pay close attention to the exact words they use to describe their problems. We will want to repeat back to them these exact words as they will feel familiar and comfortable in their minds.

The only warning is to stay focused. Don't get distracted by cat videos.

An example of YouTube.com research?

Imagine we sold legal services. Just search for "stupid laws in the world" and prepare to be humored and amazed. Insane laws, people's emotional reactions, and a wealth of fun stories we can tell our prospects.

But we might be thinking, "That is not mind reading. They didn't have those laws and concerns inside of their heads." But, they do now! And some of the stories they will never be able to get out of their heads.

RESEARCH IDEA: #9: MAGAZINES ARE IN THE BUSINESS OF APPEALING TO THE PROBLEMS AND DESIRES OF THEIR READERS' MINDS.

They interview the right people, research their topics, and analyze their findings.

Do we want to see the big picture? The biggest emotional concerns of our target market? Then look at the magazine covers, the headlines, and the hooks, that entice them to buy the magazine. Standing in front of a magazine stand can give us deep-level research in minutes.

If we sold skincare and cosmetics, this is a no-brainer.

Bring a notepad. This is what is on our target market's minds.

- "13 foods for better skin"
- "How to make your hormones work for you"
- "The perfect lipstick color to attract the ..."
- "The night-time routine that ..."

Well, we get the idea. Need proof that this is exactly what is on our target market's minds? These magazines are still in business. If no one bought these magazines, if their headlines did not interest them, there would be no money to print and distribute these magazines. Millions of dollars of research. All we have to do is read.

These headlines are easy to transition into mind reading statements. We could say, "You are probably wondering what is the best way to keep wrinkles from forming." Mind reading is easy.

RESEARCH IDEA: #10. LAST, BUT NOT LEAST, WE WON'T UNDERESTIMATE THE POWER OF A PERSON-TO-PERSON CONVERSATION.

Real conversation with a "live" human being means we can ask questions, get real-time answers, and then go deeper into the areas of interest. We might find out that our assumptions were ... just assumptions, and not facts. Who knows? Our conversation partners might tell us the one thing that keeps them awake at night. That is the nugget we will add to our mind reading inventory.

An example of a person-to-person research conversation paying off with new insights?

I thought prospects buy diet products to slim down and be healthy.

Wrong.

One day I had a conversation with a young lady. I asked her how her diet products business was doing. She complained, "I am so tired. All I do, day after day, is deliver giant boxes of diet products to customers. It is exhausting."

Well, she obviously knew something I didn't. I asked her what she did.

"Oh, I go to bridal shows," she said. "Every bride wants to lose a couple of pounds to look good in their wedding dress." That made sense to me. No wonder she could sell a box of diet products for $400. Soon-to-be-brides have motivation. But the research got better.

She continued, "But that isn't the big money. Their mothers and future mothers-in-law buy boxes and boxes. They know they will be in the wedding pictures. They don't want to look fat in those wedding pictures for the rest of their lives. The wedding will cost tens of thousands of dollars, so stocking up a few extra boxes of diet products is small change to them."

LET'S INVEST TIME IN OUR RESEARCH

We might end up knowing more about the needs and desires in our prospects' minds than they do. And of course, this gives us great mind reading powers. Our prospects will trust us and believe us. Now our message will get through loud and clear.

93

SUMMARY

Mind reading is a superpower.

Rapport is the most important skill in dealing with our prospects.

If prospects don't trust us, or believe what we say, nothing will work. Our mind reading superpower takes rapport to a much higher level. This almost seems unfair.

We can now build a direct connection with our prospects' thoughts and feelings.

They will hear our message and hear it clearly.

We won't have to fight through prejudices, objections, biases, and skepticism.

What happens when prospects hear our message loud and clear?

They have a choice.

They can choose our wonderful offer and how it will improve their lives, or they can choose to keep their lives the same.

Most will want a better life.

There is nothing mystical or supernatural about mind reading. Every human does it. The difference is that we will do it at a much higher level. How?

By listening, and then using the simple magic phrases in this book.

Now that we know the words, the next step is to practice. Getting experience will be fun, and profitable too!

The best part about getting more experience? Eventually, we will know what our prospects are going to say next, before they say it. We disable their objections before they even say them. And, we will do this with simple conversation. No rejection.

Enjoy using the shortcut phrases and watch your business grow!

—Keith & Tom

MORE FROM BIG AL BOOKS

SEE THEM ALL AT BIGALBOOKS.COM

MINDSET SERIES

Secrets to Mastering Your Mindset
Take Control of Your Network Marketing Career

Breaking the Brain Code
Easy Lessons for Your Network Marketing Career

How to Get Motivated in 60 Seconds
The Secrets to Instant Action

PROSPECTING AND RECRUITING SERIES

Overcoming Objections
Making Network Marketing Rejection-Free

Hooks! The Invisible Sales Superpower
Create Network Marketing Prospects Who Want to Know More

How to Get Appointments Without Rejection
Fill Our Calendars with Network Marketing Prospects

Create Influence
10 Ways to Impress and Guide Others

How to Meet New People Guidebook
Overcome Fear and Connect Now

How to Get Your Prospect's Attention and Keep It!
Magic Phrases for Network Marketing

10 Shortcuts Into Our Prospects' Minds
Get Network Marketing Decisions Fast!

How To Prospect, Sell And Build Your Network Marketing Business With Stories

26 Instant Marketing Ideas To Build Your Network Marketing Business

51 Ways and Places to Sponsor New Distributors
Discover Hot Prospects For Your Network Marketing Business

First Sentences for Network Marketing
How To Quickly Get Prospects On Your Side

Big Al's MLM Sponsoring Magic
How To Build A Network Marketing Team Quickly

Start SuperNetworking!
5 Simple Steps to Creating Your Own Personal Networking Group

GETTING STARTED SERIES

How to Build Your Network Marketing Business in 15 Minutes a Day

3 Easy Habits For Network Marketing
Automate Your MLM Success

Quick Start Guide for Network Marketing
Get Started FAST, Rejection-FREE!

FOUR CORE SKILLS SERIES

How To Get Instant Trust, Belief, Influence and Rapport!
13 Ways To Create Open Minds By Talking To The Subconscious Mind

Ice Breakers!
How To Get Any Prospect To Beg You For A Presentation

Pre-Closing for Network Marketing
"Yes" Decisions Before The Presentation

The Two-Minute Story for Network Marketing
Create the Big-Picture Story That Sticks!

PERSONALITY TRAINING SERIES (THE COLORS)

The Four Color Personalities for MLM
The Secret Language for Network Marketing

Mini-Scripts for the Four Color Personalities
How to Talk to our Network Marketing Prospects

Why Are My Goals Not Working?
Color Personalities for Network Marketing Success

How To Get Kids To Say Yes!
Using the Secret Four Color Languages to Get Kids to Listen

PRESENTATION AND CLOSING SERIES

Closing for Network Marketing
Getting Prospects Across The Finish Line

The One-Minute Presentation
Explain Your Network Marketing Business Like A Pro

How to Follow Up With Your Network Marketing Prospects
Turn Not Now Into Right Now!

Retail Sales for Network Marketers
How to Get New Customers for Your MLM Business

LEADERSHIP SERIES

Be the Top 1% in Network Marketing
7 Simple Steps to Leave the 99% Behind

The Complete Three-Book Network Marketing Leadership Series
Series includes: How To Build Network Marketing Leaders Volume One, How To Build Network Marketing Leaders Volume Two, and Motivation. Action. Results.

How To Build Network Marketing Leaders
Volume One: Step-By-Step Creation Of MLM Professionals

How To Build Network Marketing Leaders
Volume Two: Activities And Lessons For MLM Leaders

Motivation. Action. Results.

How Network Marketing Leaders Move Their Teams

What Smart Sponsors Do
Supercharge Our Network Marketing Team

MORE BOOKS...

Why You Need to Start Network Marketing
How to Remove Risk and Have a Better Life

How To Build Your Network Marketing Nutrition Business Fast

How Speakers, Trainers, and Coaches Get More Bookings
12 Ways to Flood Our Calendars with Paid Events

How To Build Your Network Marketing Utilities Business Fast

Getting "Yes" Decisions
What insurance agents and financial advisors can say to clients

Public Speaking Magic
Success and Confidence in the First 20 Seconds

Worthless Sponsor Jokes
Network Marketing Humor

ABOUT THE AUTHORS

Keith Schreiter has 30+ years of experience in network mar-keting and MLM. He shows network marketers how to use simple systems to build a stable and growing business.

So, do you need more prospects? Do you need your prospects to commit instead of stalling? Want to know how to engage and keep your group active? If these are the types of skills you would like to master, you will enjoy his "how-to" style.

Keith speaks and trains in the U.S., Canada, and Europe.

Tom "Big Al" Schreiter has 50+ years of experience in network marketing and MLM. As the author of the original "Big Al" training books in the late '70s, he has continued to speak in over 80 countries on using the exact words and phrases to get prospects to open up their minds and say "YES."

His passion is marketing ideas, marketing campaigns, and how to speak to the subconscious mind in simplified, practical ways. He is always looking for case studies of incredible marketing campaigns that give usable lessons.

As the author of numerous audio trainings, Tom is a favorite speaker at company conventions and regional events.